ESCAPE
THE
ORDINARY

DEVOTIONALS

C. Mitchell

CAMERON GRACE MITCHELL

www.xulonpress.com

In loving memory of my sweet grandmother, Pasty
Ann Mitchell, who lived out the *fruits of the Spirit*:
joy, peace, patience, kindness, goodness, faithful-
ness, gentleness, self-control, and the greatest she
demonstrated was love.

TABLE OF CONTENTS

LIGHT OF THE WORLD

Devotion of the day: I hope you have a day full of peace and love. Remember that God is always with you, no matter what: that is amazing grace and true love. Jesus died for us so that we can have a relationship with Him. How amazing is that? He would trade the whole creation to win our affections back. Wow. The love of God is all you need. What should we do with this crazy love? We should reflect it through our actions and words, to lead others closer to Christ. When people see the Lord's light through us, they will want that light, too. Isn't that our purpose on earth? God called us to be a light in this dark, broken world and further His kingdom.

Challenge of the day: Be kind to someone that may be hard for you to love, and be a refection of Jesus's light.

Verse of the day: Matthew 5:14 (NIV)~"You are the light of the world. A city on a hill cannot be hidden."

Prayer of the day: Dear God, please help me look like your love as long as I live. Let me love like you love everyone, even when it's challenging. Thank you for dying on the cross for my sins, because you loved me. I am forever grateful. In Jesus's name, I pray. Amen.

ORDINARY OR EXTRAORDINARY?

Devotion of the day: You have twenty-four hours today. How are you going to spend it? Will you stress about things you cannot control, be concerned with what people think about you, or worry how many followers you have on social network? Those distractions are from the enemy. He wants us to distance ourselves from God and even forget Him. Well, that's not what the Lord desires for you to do. Do not put your focus on the things of this world. Keep your attention on God: resist those temptations. When we turn our eyes away from worthless things, we will leap into our relationships with Christ. To chose to value time according to God's standards takes maturity, and helps us protect our hearts and become more like Him. What you do with the hours you have been given shows what kind of person you are, and determines what kind of person you will become. *Ordinary or Extraordinary:* which will you be?

Challenge of the day: Pray that God will make you revolutionary, and ask that your focus will be on pursuing Him.

Verse of the day: Psalm 119:37 (NIV)~"Turn my eyes away from worthless things; preserve my life according to your word."

Prayer of the day: Dear God, please transform me into a revolutionary Christian who is on fire for you. In Jesus's name, I pray. Amen.

YOU ARE A CHILD OF GOD

Devotion of the day: How much your clothes cost does not define who you are. How many friends you have does not define who you are. What kind of grades you receive does not define who you are. *You are a child of God:* that defines you. You are a part of Christ, and you are worth more than all of creation. You are God's most prized possession. You belong to Him, and nothing else matters. Sometimes we need to be reminded who we are. We are God's beloveds; all we have to do is believe it. We get caught up in how we look or how we perform a sport or activity, but belonging to Christ is the most important thing in the world. Remember whose you are: you are God's.

Challenge of the day: Listen to the song "Remind Me Who I Am" by Jason Gray.

Verse of the day: Song of Solomon 2:16 (NIV)~"My beloved is mine and I am His."

Prayer of the day: Dear God, please help me to comprehend that I belong to you and not the world. Let me feel Your presence and unfailing love today. In Jesus's name, I pray. Amen.

ON FIRE FOR JESUS

Devotion of the day: Love is very powerful. Think of the person or thing that you treasure the very most, then multiply that by a number bigger than you can comprehend. That would represent the power of God's love for you. His kind of love has the ability to stay, no matter what kind of person you have become. There is no trouble that can cause God to run from you. God's love burns like a blazing fire: He cannot keep His eyes off you. *He's crazy about you!* When His love becomes the thing we live for, it creates a fire in our lives. It is a passion that gives our lives purpose. He becomes the reason for the decisions we make and everything we do. You need more to live for: Jesus is that thing. Be on fire for His unending love.

Challenge of the day: Say this prayer: "Dear God, set a fire inside of me. May you be

the one thing that I live for. Amen."

Verse of the day: Song of Solomon 8:6-7 (NIV)~ "Place me like a seal over your heart, like a seal on your arm. For love is as strong as death, its jealousy as enduring as the grave. Love flashes like fire, the brightest kind of flame. Many waters cannot quench love, nor can rivers drown it. If a man tried to buy love with all his wealth, his offer would be utterly scorned."

Prayer of the day: Dear God, thank you for loving me unconditionally. Please help me to change lives through this love. In Jesus's name, I pray. Amen.

PEACE BE WITH YOU

Devotion of the day: You must be worn: from the stresses of school, trying to have stable relationships, maybe worrying about your performance in sports or activities, and many other obligations and responsibilities. God will give you rest. He will take all your anxiety away from you. All you have to do is pray, and trust that God is always with you and cares for you. Even when you feel like you cannot take life anymore, remember that you will never be alone and God will give you peace through His presence. He is our refuge and strength: we can do all things through Him. When you are needy for unconditional love, and you need help, breathe this simple prayer: *Jesus, I need you.* God sees your worries and longs to take them away from you. The Lord says, "Peace be with you." Let go, and let God handle it. He has you in His arms.

Challenge of the day: Squeeze your hands together, as tightly as you can, like you're praying. Think of the thing that is troubling you. Let go of your hands, and imagine God taking that trouble away from you.

Verse of the day: 1 Peter 5:7 (NIV)~"Cast all your anxiety on him because he cares for you."

Prayer of the day: Dear God, I give you my worries and fears. Jesus, I need you. In Jesus's name, I pray. Amen.

GOD KNOWS WHAT HE'S DOING

Devotion of the day: God's timing is perfect: it is not too soon nor delayed. In its perfection, trusting in His timing of things is important to understand. He knew you before you were even formed in your mother's womb. He has your whole life planned out. There is no need for you to worry about it! God has it under control: He will carry you through your obstacles and your wonderful moments, too. God is there through it all and has you in His perfect embrace. When something doesn't go the way you planned, remember that God created it that way. He meant for that to happen for a purpose. With God, nothing is a coincidence: everything happens for a reason.

Challenge of the day: Write down the plans and dreams you hope to see come true. Pray over these things, and give God control.

Verse of the day: Jeremiah 29:11 (NIV)~"For I know the plans I have for you, declares the Lord. Plans to prosper you, not to harm you. Plans to give you a hope and a future."

Prayer of the day: Dear God, please help me trust that you are in control and that your plans are perfect. In Jesus's name, I pray. Amen.

GOD IS FREEDOM

Devotion of the day: We might think that God is a rule-making God: but God is not about making rules, and being a Christian isn't about all the things we shouldn't do. Living for Jesus is about living freely. You were a captive of sin, but you were set free by Jesus's blood and love for you. Jesus died on the cross so we can all live full lives. The Christian life isn't boring! Let God use you; do great things: go live life to the fullest, for His glory.

Challenge of the day: Do something extraordinary today, whether it is big or small.

{Examples: being respectful to a teacher, telling your parents how much you appreciate them, having a positive attitude, praying for others, etc...}

Verse of the day: 1 Peter 2:16 (NIV)~ "Live as free men, but do not use your freedom as a cover-up for evil; live as servants of God."

Prayer of the day: Dear God, thank you for setting me free from sin. In Jesus's name, I pray. Amen.

MASTER OF THE STORMS

Devotion of the day: Storms often arise quickly in our lives. The trials we face test us; we have the opportunity to turn these results into new confidence and strength. Jesus didn't promise that the trip would be easy. He just wants us to put our trust in Him during this time. Even in the worst storms, it will bring us new wisdom and, ultimately, unflinching hope in the Lord, if we trust that He is working in us. Jesus is right beside us, offering comfort and a way out, even through the most out-of-control storms.

Challenge of the day: Thank God in the calm and in the storm. Give thanks always and in all situations.

Verse of the day: Mark 4:38-39 {The Message}~ "The disciples roused him, saying, 'Teacher, is it nothing to you that we're going down?' 'Awake now,' he told the wind to pipe down and said to the sea, 'Quiet! Settle down!' The wind ran out of breath; the sea became smooth as glass. Jesus reprimanded the disciples, 'Why are you such cowards? Don't you have any faith at all?'

Prayer of the day: Dear God, when trials arise, please let me remember that it is part of your plan for a reason and that I am supposed to learn something from this. In Jesus's name, I pray. Amen.

エ

HIS BEAUTIFUL MASTERPIECE

Devotion of the day: You are beautiful: you are intelligent: you are kind. You are worth more than you could ever imagine, because of a Savior who died to know you and to have a relationship with you. You are His beloved; you are His darling: you are His masterpiece. Nothing in the world could separate you from His kind of love: it is reckless for us. He will never ever stop loving you. Jesus thinks you are beautiful: He loves your outsides and insides. Every part of your being was fashioned by the Creator of the universe. How amazing is that? When He looks at you, Jesus sees the child He created. He sees the little one He died for; the masterpiece He is passionate about. *You are fearfully and wonderfully made.*

Challenge of the day: Look in the mirror and say, "Jesus thinks I'm beautiful!"

Verse of the day: Song of Solomon 6:10 {The Message}~ "Has anyone ever seen anything like this dawn-fresh, moon-lovely, sun-radiant, ravishing as the night sky with its galaxies of stars {That's you}?"

Prayer of the day: Dear God, please help me to feel beautiful because you created me. In Jesus's name, I pray. Amen.

LOVE THE LORD WITH ALL YOUR HEART

Devotion of the day: Sometimes you may feel like you disappoint God: you don't. He loves you, no matter what you do: that's unconditional love and everlasting forgiveness. You don't have to do good deeds to win God's approval. All He wants is your heart. He wants you to love Him with all your heart and wants you to get to know Him. The reason why you should do good deeds is because God lives within you. All the glory should go to Him, not you. Have the right motive when you do something good. Do it for God, and let Him have your heart and every part of you.

Challenge of the day: If you haven't accepted Jesus into your heart, do it right now.

Verse of the day: Luke 10:27 (NIV)~ "Love the Lord your God with all your heart, with all your soul, with all your mind, and with all your strength."

Prayer of the day: Dear God, please help me to love you with my full heart, and please change my perspective so that I don't have to win Your approval, because You already love me. In Jesus's name, I pray. Amen.

JESUS IS A FRIEND

Devotion of the day: Submit yourself to God: read His word, pray, listen for Him speaking to you, and give your mind over to Him. When you do these simple things, the devil will leave your path and you will draw closer to God. Learning more about the Lord will help you become more like Him. Learn about God like you study for a test: read the Bible, and learn about His love and everything else He is. You will be renewed when doing so.

Challenge of the day: Try to be closer with God and read His word more.

Verse of the day: James 4:8 (NIV)~ "Come near to God and He will come near to you."

Prayer of the day: Dear God, I submit myself to you. I am all yours. In Jesus's name, I pray. Amen.

THINK BEFORE YOU SPEAK

Devotion of the day: The words you say have a big impact on those around you. Sometimes words make you happy, but sometimes they make you feel insecure or upset. Before you speak, think:

Is what you are saying helpful?
Is it kind?
Will it make the person feel good?
Is it important or just gossip?
Will it glorify God?

Remember this before you speak, and it will help filter your words. If you have nothing nice to say, don't say it! If you are overwhelmed with the Holy Spirit, and you want to make someone's day with a kind comment, do it right now. What you say can save a life or hurt a life. Pray, and ask God to give you the discernment to know what to say and what not to say.

Challenge of the day: Try to go through the whole day without gossiping.

Verse of the day: Ephesians 4:29 (NIV)~ "Do not let any unwholesome talk come out of your mouth, but only what is helpful for building others up according to their needs, that it may benefit those who listen."

Prayer of the day: Dear God, please help me choose my words wisely. Help me to

say things that are kind and encouraging. Please give me better judgment. In Jesus's name, I pray. Amen.

BE CAREFUL, LITTLE EYES

Devotion of the day: Be careful what your little eyes see. Be careful what your little ears hear. We live in a broken world where there is sin everywhere: for example, what you choose to read, what television or movies you choose to watch, or what music you choose to listen to. You need to be cautious on what you see and hear. Your body is where the Lord lives: you need to let holy thoughts and things into it. Also, the things you are exposed to make you who you are. If you are around many bad words, you may start repeating them. If you watch inappropriate movies or see inappropriate things, those things are permanently in your mind. So, steer clear of these sinful things: they are from the devil, trying to make you distance yourself from God's love.

Challenge of the day: Try a social media fasting. It's only five days, and you don't use any social media, including Twitter, Instagram, Facebook, Vine, or Snapchat...etc. By doing this, you will hear from God.

Verse of the day: Proverbs 4:23 (NIV)~"Above all else, guard your heart, for everything you do flows from it."

Prayer of the day: Dear God, please help me be mindful what I watch and listen to. In Jesus's name, I pray. Amen.

GOD IS BIGGER

Devotion of the day: We are the children of God, and we need to understand that God's love will protect us from everything. He is much bigger and much more powerful than any of our fears. All we have to do is put our faith in Him. God is our father, who shelters us with His huge wings and keeps us safe from evil in this world. His warmth comforts our souls under His powerful and gracious presence; He comforts us under our tribulations, as well as defends us from the enemy. Sometimes being a Christian is overwhelming, and sometimes a little scary, but if you hand over all your anxiety to Him, He will give you strength and peace with His presence.

Challenge of the day: Close your eyes and imagine God holding you in His lap, while He is comforting you and stroking your hair. You will feel peace.

Verse of the day: Psalm 91:4 (NIV)~ "He will cover you with his feathers. He will shelter you with his wings. His faithful promises are your armor and protection."

Prayer of the day: Dear God, please help me to feel Your presence, and let me understand that you are bigger than any of my fears or trials. In Jesus's name, I pray. Amen.

GREEN WITH ENVY

Devotion of the day: Comparing ourselves to others is something I think we are all guilty of: sometimes we do it without thinking. However, God created you to be you and no one else. God created you for a purpose only you can accomplish. When you are content with whom God made you to be, you will be positive and happier. Envy exhausts you and is a waste of energy: pray to God if you are struggling with this. Remember that God created you perfectly and in His image!

Challenge of the day: Think of five things that you like about yourself, and thank God for those things.

Verse of the day: Proverbs 14:30 (NIV)~"A heart at peace gives life to the body, but envy rots the bones."

Prayer of the day: Dear God, please help me to not compare myself to others, and to be confident in whom You created me to be. In Jesus's name, I pray. Amen.

PERFECTLY IMPERFECT

Devotion of the day: We aren't perfect. We can try our very best to do what's right, but we still make mistakes: it's just in our nature. However, Jesus is perfect. It's hard to understand and fathom how Christ loves us unconditionally. Even in our messes, He loves us and cares for us. Because of our imperfections Christ died on the cross, so that we could be perfected through the perfect one. He didn't die for us because He had to: He died for us because He wanted to. Jesus desired to have a relationship with us, even when we disobeyed Him and fall short. His love is perfect, and God loves you perfectly and all your imperfections.

Challenge of the day: Don't worry and let go of your past mistakes.

Verse of the day: Romans 5:8 (NIV)~"But God demonstrates his own love for us in this: While we were still sinners, Christ died for us."

Prayer of the day: Dear God, thank you for loving me, even when I betray you and make mistakes. In Jesus's name, I pray. Amen.

HIS LOVE WILL REMAIN

Devotion of the day: God can work everything out. Remain attentive to Him, and let God guide you through your choices. Do not give up: have hope in the Lord, no matter what situation you are in. If you are weary, just approach it as an opportunity to turn to God's strength. Remember that God makes everything good. Sometimes it is hard to understand what God is doing in your life, but just trust that His will and plan is perfect. Even in the hardest circumstance, God uses that event to help you grow in your relationship with Him, so you can rely on Him in the toughest times.

Challenge of the day: Memorize Romans 8:28.

Verse of the day: Romans 8:28 (NIV)~"And we know that in all things God works for the good of those who love him, who have been called according to his purpose."

Prayer of the day: Dear God, help me to rely on you in the toughest times. In Jesus's name, I pray. Amen.

DREAM FOR YOU

Devotion of the day: God has a dream for you. He imagined a wonderful plan and purpose for your life, so you could lead others to Him from your story. We have dreams and hopes of our own; however, God may have something better in mind. We may think we have it all figured out, but we really don't know what to do with our lives: what college to go to, what job to have, whom to marry, and many other questions that the answers are uncertain. Believe that God has everything under control and will lead you to the right decision. Be willing to change your plans as well, if it is God's will. If you feel God pushing you towards something, don't ignore it; go for it!

Challenge of the day: Listen for God speaking to you.

Verse of the day: Philippians 3:14 {The Message}~ "I'm not saying that I have this all together, that I have it made. But I am well on my way, reaching out for Christ, who has so wondrously reached out for me. Friends, don't get me wrong: By no means do I count myself an expert in all of this, but I've got my eye on the goal, where God is beckoning us onward—to Jesus. I'm off and running, and I'm not turning back."

Prayer of the day: Dear God, I give all my dreams and plans to you. I'll do whatever you'd like: it's the least I can do. In Jesus's name, I pray. Amen.

PATIENCE

Devotion of the day: Patience: probably one of the hardest fruits of the spirit to most people. Being patient by definition is: "the quality of being patient, as the bearing of provocation, annoyance, misfortune, or pain, without complaint, loss of temper, irritation, or the like" (Webster.com). Having patience is very important, because God tells us in His word to love your neighbor. He didn't say be kind to those who are easy to be kind to. God tells us to love each other in brotherly love, and He tells us to love those who are harder to love. Strive to be patient in every situation, even when it is difficult. You'll be pointing your patience towards God, which will inspire others to have tolerance as well.

Challenge of the day: Try to be patient all day.

Verse of the day: John 13:34-35 (NIV)~"A new commandment I give to you, that you love one another: just as I have loved you, you also are to love one another. By this all people will know that you are my disciples, if you have love for one another."

Prayer of the day: Dear God, today, give me your patience and mercy for others. In Jesus's name, I pray. Amen.

GOD IS LOVE

Devotion of the day: Today is the day to celebrate God's love. There is nothing in all creation that is more powerful than God's everlasting love. He loves us no matter what: His unconditional love is something we can never really comprehend. In His holiness, He still desires to have a relationship with His children, even when we are sinners. No earthly thing is like God's love for each and every one of us. God thinks we are worth dying on the cross and being beaten for: that is how powerful His love is for us. Praise God and His love that is never-ending. We may never fully understand His love for us, but we need to believe it and be thankful.

Challenge of the day: Thank God for everything He has done for you.

Verse of the day: Ephesians 3:18 (NIV)~ "May I have power, together with all the Lord's holy people, to grasp how wide and long and high and deep is the love of Christ."

Prayer of the day: Dear God, thank you so much for everything you have done for me. I am truly blessed. In Jesus's name, I pray. Amen.

MADE TO BE COURAGEOUS

Devotion of the day: We were created to lead others to Christ: doing so takes courage. Sometimes it is a little intimidating to talk to nonbelievers about our faith and beliefs. Even just talking to our friends about God may make us feel uncomfortable. God will give us the confidence to do it. All we have to do is actually tell others the good news. You don't have to do something big. Start to just talk about Jesus in your normal conversation with your friends and family. The more you practice, the more comfortable you will be talking to others about God. Then, you will be able to speak truth to everyone you encounter, which is our purpose here on earth.

Challenge of the day: Talk about Jesus to your friends or family.

Verse of the day: Deuteronomy 31:6 {NLV} ~"Be strong and have strength of heart. Do not be afraid or shake with fear because of them. For the Lord your God is the One Who goes with you. He will be faithful to you. He will not leave you alone."

Prayer of the day: Dear God, please give me the courage to talk about your powerful ways. Let it not be my words, but your words through me to reach out for your glory. I want your courage to do what I feel you are calling me to do. In Jesus's name, I pray. Amen.

UNFLINCHING SHELTER

Devotion of the day: When you encounter a difficult situation, you think to yourself, "How am I going to get through this?" In these circumstances, you quickly learn how strong, how faithful, and how capable God truly is. When you overcome something that you never thought you could, know that God is working in your life. With Christ, everything is possible. Never lose hope, because God can do anything. He will provide for you and give you strength when you are weak.

Challenge of the day: Look up a Bible verse about hope.

Verse of the day: Isaiah 40:31 (NIV)~"But those who hope in the LORD will renew their strength. They will soar on wings like eagles; they will run and not grow weary, they will walk and not be faint."

Prayer of the day: Dear God, with you everything is possible. Please help me to believe that. In Jesus's name, I pray. Amen.

LIVE BY FAITH

Devotion of the day: Having faith in God's existence is something that takes time. It's hard to understand that there is a God who created everything not only in the world, but the entire universe. This God also made you: He planned out your whole life and knows everything about you. This concept may never be fully understood; however, that's what makes God so amazing. We will never know every single detail about Him. That's why we need to keep pursuing Christ: there is always something to learn. We can't see Him or physically touch Him, but we can feel His presence: we can see His fingerprints in creation, and we can witness His miracles.

Challenge of the day: Look for God's fingerprints all around you. For example, nature, a miracle, the Bible, and much more.

Verse of the day: 2 Corinthians 5:7 (NIV)~ "For we live by faith, not by sight."

Prayer of the day: Dear God, give me faith in you and all that you are about. Please help me to feel confident in you, and please help me not to have any doubts. In Jesus's name, I pray. Amen.

JESUS LOVED YOU FIRST

Devotion of the day: Loving someone is a lot easier when you know you are loved back. Well, God loves you greatly, so you need to spread that love around to everyone. Return the love of God to someone who may not deserve it, but needs it. Christ's love should overflow within your heart. God's love should spill and touch others. Love, because He first loved you.

Challenge of the day: Love someone today because Jesus loved you first.

Verse of the day: 1 John 4:19 (NIV)~"We love because he first loved us."

Prayer of the day: Dear God, since you have poured into me, please help me to pour into others with Your love. In Jesus's name, I pray. Amen.

BE JOYFUL ALWAYS

Devotion of the day: Happiness is a choice: we choose if we want to be joyful or not. Situations we are put into should not change our attitudes. Be positive. When doing so, life will be so much brighter and more enjoyable. Life is way too short to be unhappy: there is always something good in a bad day. You may not realize it right away, but remember that God is there in control. Remember that, "this is the day that the Lord has made. Rejoice and be glad in it" (Psalm 118:24).

Challenge of the day: Try to look at the positives all day.

Verse of the day: 1 Thessalonians 5:16-18 (NIV)~"Be joyful always, pray without ceasing, give thanks in all circumstances; for this is the will of God in Christ Jesus for you."

Prayer of the day: Dear God, help me to focus on today and to not be negative. Let me be joyful always. In Jesus's name, I pray. Amen.

LOVE YOU BACK

Devotion of the day: God can take our shame and imperfections and make us new. With His love and mercy, we become something beautiful. He washed all our sins away with His precious blood over thousands of years ago. The least we can do is serve Him and love Him back.

Challenge of the day: Love God back today.

Verse of the day: 2 Corinthians 5:17 (NIV)~"Therefore, if anyone is in Christ, the new creation has come: The old has gone, the new has come."

Prayer of the day: Dear God, I love you so much. In Jesus's name, I pray. Amen.

TABLE FOR TWO

Devotion of the day: We have such busy and crazy schedules: from school, sports, activities, and other numerous responsibilities and obligations. We seem to have time for all of that, but not for God. We say, "I'll pray tomorrow," "I'll read my Bible later," or "I don't have time to spend time with God today." Sometimes we are treating God like He is not important or worthy enough to be a part of our lives. If you feel this way, pray to Jesus. Pray to God to make Him your number one priority and focus. Don't go astray and away from God. Pray and as you are pursuing Him, He will come to you and give you peace.

Challenge of the day: Have some one-on-one quiet time with God today.

Verse of the day: Matthew 6:6 (NIV)~"But when you pray, go into your room and shut the door and pray to your Father who is in secret. And your Father who sees in secret will reward you."

Prayer of the day: Dear God, please help me to make you my number one priority. Help me to spend more quiet time with you. In Jesus's name, I pray. Amen.

WHO CAN STOP US?

Devotion of the day: If God is within you, nothing can stop you. He will get you through everything and anything that life throws at you. When you think you have failed at something (maybe did bad on a test, made a mistake in a sport, or felt like you weren't good enough), remember that God is with you all the time and what you think is a failure is actually an opportunity to grow. You cannot fail. Read that again. God is so in love with you that He lives inside of you and gives you strength to do anything you put your mind to. If God is for us, who can stop us?

Challenge of the day: Be confident that God is with you and that you are not a failure.

Verse of the day: Psalms 46:5 (NIV)~ God is within {him/her}. {He/She} will not fail.

Prayer of the day: Dear God, no one can stop me because you live within me. Help me to remember that in challenging times. In Jesus's name, I pray. Amen.

LEAD ME SO I CAN LEAD

Devotion of the day: We need leaders of Christ. We need people to lead others to Christ in everything they do. You can do that. If we don't have leaders in His world, then there are no followers: and we need followers in Christ to further His kingdom. Being a leader may seem intimidating, and an act you can't complete, but everyone is capable. Faith is not meant to be done alone: we need to work together as the body of Christ. God will lead us to become leaders for Him.

Challenge of the day: Start today to be a leader and example of Christ.

Verse of the day: Proverbs 16:9 (NIV)~ "The heart of man plans his way, but the Lord establishes his steps."

Prayer of the day: Dear God, lead me, so I can lead others to Your kingdom. I can't do it without you. In Jesus's name, I pray. Amen.

YOU CAN CHANGE THE WORLD

Devotion of the day: Some people think that teen-agers can't make a difference. They think they are too young or not mature enough, but the Bible tells us otherwise. It doesn't matter how old you are, you can still make an impact on the world. Don't let anyone tell you different. Be confident in who you are and the relationship you have with Christ. When you do that, nothing can stop you from changing the world for the better.

Challenge of the day: Think of a way that you can change the world for the better.

Verse of the day: 1 Timothy 4:12 (NIV)~ "Don't let anyone look down on you because you are young, but set an example for the believers in speech, in life, in love, in faith and in purity."

Prayer of the day: Dear God, please give me the strength and confidence to make a difference. Big or small actions of Your love can impact the whole world. Please help me to put Your acts of love into action. In Jesus's name, I pray. Amen.

PRESS ON TOWARD THE GOAL

Devotion of the day: We can't keep dwelling on our mistakes, or they will keep replaying in our minds until they are all we see. Today, when you feel like the devil is taking control of your life, and trying to pull you down in your attitude so that you can't glorify the Lord, just remember to fix your eyes on Jesus. Everyone is going to make a mistake at some point: it's inescapable. However, He doesn't care if you mess up, as long as you give your all for Him. The Lord is making all things new! Look forward to your goal, forget past mistakes and look for a new opportunity to come to you. Trust that God will give you the determination, strength, focus, and endurance to accomplish your dreams and aspirations.

Challenge of the day: Let go of your past regrets and mistakes.

Verse of the day: Philippians 3:13-14 (NIV)~"Forgetting what is behind and straining toward what is ahead, I press on toward the goal to win the prize for which God has called me heavenward in Christ Jesus."

Prayer of the day: Dear God, please help me to let go of my past mistakes, guilt, and regret. Thank you for wiping my record clean, when I did not deserve it. In Jesus's name, I pray. Amen.

FREE TO BE ME

Devotion of the day: It is a challenge to accept yourself for who you are: the key is realizing the Ultimate Designer has made you. When you realize this, you are acknowledging that you have worth and value that goes beyond your physical appearance. God looks at the beauties of your heart and loves every single, little detail of you. Every part of you–from your hair color, to your personality, to your talents–is all part of His plan.

Challenge of the day: Love yourself for who you are.

Verse of the day: Psalms 138:8 (NIV)~ "The Lord will vindicate me; your love, Lord, endures forever—do not abandoned the works of your hands."

Prayer of the day: Dear God, please help me to love myself for who I am. In Jesus's name, I pray. Amen.

DO NOT FEAR, FOR I AM WITH YOU

Devotion of the day: There are a lot of scary and intimidating things in the world: life-changing decisions and much, much more. What scares you? A test, your safety, your appearance? As a Christian, there really is nothing for us to be afraid of. Jesus is on our team: He is God. The most important thing is for us to believe in Him. When we feel overwhelmed with worry or fear, pray to God. Fear does not come from the Lord; fear comes from the enemy. God will give you the peace and comfort you want and need.

Challenge of the day: Scared? Pray.

Verse of the day: Isaiah 41:10 (NIV)~"So do not fear, for I am with you; do not be dismayed, for I am your God. I will strengthen you and help you; I will uphold you with my righteous right hand."

Prayer of the day: Dear God, thank you for everything you have done for me. The worry and fear that I have in my heart, please remove it and help me feel Your living presence. Let me not hear the devil's voice, but let me hear Your voice to guide me and give me comfort. Thank you for this day You have made, and please overwhelm me with Your love. In Jesus's name, I pray. Amen.

OUR PROTECTOR

Devotion of the day: God is our protector. In a way, He is like a mighty and strong lion: we are His precious cubs. There is danger all around. The danger is the enemy and sin. Our father lion roars and casts the evil away from us. He lives in us, and that same roar is inside of us as well. We are capable of driving out evil from our hearts and minds. The devil trembles when we roar to get away from sin and closer to God. Satan goes away and is not present in our lives. Be God's lion cub today, and roar when you notice sin is creeping into your life. Be still and know that God will protect you.

Challenge of the day: Use your roar, and watch out for evil.

Verse of the day: Exodus 14:14 (NIV)~ "The Lord will fight for you; you need only to be still."

Prayer of the day: Dear God, please help me realize right from wrong. Help me to see when I am living in sin. When this happens, help me to cast sin and evil away from my heart and mind, so I can live for you. In Jesus's name, I pray. Amen.

PRAYER IS POWERFUL

Devotion of the day: Pray: sometimes this action is hard. We don't know what to pray for or how to pray. The thing about praying is that God already knows what's going on. You pray, so you can feel peace talking to God about your situation. That's the amazing part about praying, so do it more often. Prayer is so powerful. Also, it doesn't matter where you are: you can pray anywhere at anytime.

Challenge of the day: Try to pray at least five times today and see what God does.

Verse of the day: 1 Thessalonians 5:17 (NIV)~ "Pray continually."

Prayer of day: Dear God, please help me go to You in trouble and joy. Let me pray to have a stronger bond with You. Light a fire in me. Set me ablaze to pray to You. Please help me pray more than I am right now. God, let You help me to pray for decisions, comfort, and everyday life. In Jesus's name, I pray. Amen.

HIS LOVE ENDURES FOREVER & HE IS ENOUGH

Devotion of the day: We are so incredibly blessed, but sometimes we take it for granted. We get so caught up in getting the next big thing. We get consumed and want more and more stuff; however, it's never enough. God is more than enough. He will satisfy you and fill your emptiness. The love that God has for us is wonderful and priceless. The earthly things we focus on don't last: Jesus, however, lasts for eternity.

Challenge of the day: Try to go the whole day being thankful for what you have, and try not to complain about what you don't have.

Verse of the day: Psalm 107:1 (NIV)~ "Oh give thanks to the Lord, for he is good, His love endures forever!"

Prayer of the day: Dear God, thank you so much for everything you have blessed me with. Please help me appreciate those things. Be my one and only fulfillment. Let me not focus on earthly things, but only focus on my relationship with you. In Jesus's name, I pray. Amen.

STOP AND LISTEN

Devotion of the day: When we ask God for clarity, or an answer to a difficult situation, we fail to stop and listen for His response and guidance. We must be willing to pause and hear Him speak to us. This waiting period may be a moment, days, months, or even years to final hear His voice. God provides us each day with His wisdom to face decisions. The question is, "Am I willing to slow down my busy schedule to quiet down to hear from my Heavenly Father?"

Challenge of the day: Take time out of your day to be still and quiet to listen for God's voice.

Verse of the day: Psalm 37:4-5 (NIV)~ "Delight yourself in the Lord, and he will give you the desires of your heart. Commit your way to the Lord; trust in him, and he will act."

Prayer of the day: Dear God, I want to hear you, but sometimes I am too focused on other responsibilities. Teach me to slow down and listen to you. In Jesus's name, I pray. Amen.

YOU LIVE FOR CHRIST

Devotion of the day: You represent Christ: this is a big responsibility and honor. You represent the Creator of the universe. You represent His love. Be filled with the Holy Spirit, and make it your goal to glorify God in everything you do. You live for Christ, not your own selfish desires. Work hard for Christ and not for others. Jesus died for you: the least you can do is live for Him.

Challenge of the day: Live for Christ.

Verse of the day: Colossians 3:23 (NIV)~ "Servants, do what you're told by your earthly masters. And don't just do the minimum that will get you by. Do your best. Work from the heart for your real Master, for God, confident that you'll get paid in full when you come into your inheritance. Keep in mind always that the ultimate Master you're serving is Christ. The sullen servant who does shoddy work will be held responsible. Being a follower of Jesus doesn't cover up bad work."

Prayer of the day: Dear God, please help me to live for you. In Jesus's name, I pray. Amen.

OVERCOME EVIL

Devotion of the day: Evil is all around us each and every day. Instead of repaying that evil with evil, do what is right and do what would glorify God: sometimes this is not easy. We get angry or upset about something and sin out of frustration; however, instead of responding with more sin, overcome evil with good. Take the high road and be the bigger person in the situation. Control your emotions. God will see that and will be proud of you. Do it all for the glory of God. Overcome evil with a victory of good and love.

Challenge of the day: Before you do something or say something, think to yourself, "What would Jesus do?"

Verse of the day: Romans 12:21 (NIV)~ "Do not be overcome by evil, but overcome evil with good."

Prayer of the day: Dear God, please help me control my emotions today. Help me to do the right thing, even when it is difficult to do so. Let all that I do point back to Your love. May I be a light in the darkness. Today, help me overcome evil with good. In Jesus's name, I pray. Amen.

HE MUST BECOME GREATER

Devotion of the day: What are the three most important things in your life, as of right now? Think about it. Was one of those things your relationship with the Lord? If not, what can you do to make God your number one priority? Don't think about yourself. We are selfish human beings, and we are always focused on what we want. However, it is not about us; it's about giving glory to God and furthering His kingdom. The devil tries to get you to think selfishly, but you need to live as you would live for the Lord. In all that you do, may it reflect His love.

Challenge of the day: Make God your reason to live.

Verse of the day: John 3:30 (NIV)~ "He must become greater; I must become less. "

Prayer of the day: Dear God, sometimes I get so caught up in what I want or what I need that I don't focus on You. Please help me make you my number one priority. Help me to glorify You in everything I do. In Jesus's name, I pray.

Amen.

JUDGMENT

Devotion of the day: Judging others is something that we do. We think of a person that sins a certain way, and we believe that we are better because we don't sin that certain sin; however, all sin is worth the same. From God's view, looking down at us like looking down at skyscrapers, all sin is the same height. One sin is not worse than another. So, we should not compare our sins to others, and we should not judge. We are all sinners, so instead of judging, we should encourage each other.

Challenge of the day: Try to not judge others today.

Verse of the day: John 8:7 (NIV)~ "When they kept on questioning him, he straightened up and said to them, 'Let any one of you who is without sin be the first to throw a stone at her.'"

Prayer of the day: Dear God, please help me not be quick to judge others on how they sin. Remind me that I am guilty of the same. Forgive my sins, and transform my crimson sins to white as snow.

GREAT IS YOUR REWARD IN HEAVEN

Devotion of the day: You may be at some point in your spiritual walk that people will bring you down because of your beliefs. When this happens, be strong and do not deny God. Trust that God will give you the wisdom and words to say to honor Him. They are only persecuting you because they see something different about you and don't understand. Be the light of the world and show others His love, even if they are unkind.

Challenge of the day: Even when people insult you, be kind. Also, be strong in your faith.

Verse of the day: Mathew 5:11 (NIV)~ "Blessed are you when people insult you, persecute you and falsely say all kinds of evil against you because of me. Rejoice and be glad, because great is your reward in heaven, for in the same way they persecuted the prophets who were before you."

Prayer of the day: Dear God, when nonbelievers are rude and treat me unkindly because of my relationship with You, please help me act like You would and handle the situation gracefully. Give me the words you want them to hear. Help me to be strong and wise. In Jesus's name, I pray. Amen.

GO TO GOD

Devotion of the day: With so much going on in our lives, sometimes we feel overwhelmed and out of sorts because we can't focus on God. To feel peace, go to God for rest. He will provide anything you need, like strength, love, faith, and much much more. Jesus will never give you something you can't handle. God loves you so much and desires for you to be happy. Go to Him for everything: He will provide always. Dig deep into His word, and you will feel His perfect presence.

Challenge of the day: Tired? Unfulfilled? Go to God today.

Verse of the day: Matthew 11:28-30 (NIV)~ "Come to me, all who are weary and burdened, and I will give you rest. Take my yoke upon you and learn from me, for I am gentle and humble in heart, and you will find rest for your souls. For my yoke is easy and my burden is light."

Prayer of the day: Dear God, today I go to you for peace and rest. In Jesus's name, I pray. Amen.

KEEP YOUR EYES OPEN

Devotion of the day: Satan wants to defeat, discourage, and destroy us. His attacks are not just willy-nilly attempts to trip us up or knock us down: he wants to take us out. He doesn't want us anywhere near God. That's why you need to be prepared and look out for his tricks; but God will protect you and help you defend yourself against the enemy. You will not go through it alone. God will be with you, no matter what. Satan understands that God lives within us; that is his motive. He strives to dim our light. Be strong and be on the lookout for the enemy's temptations and lies.

Challenge of the day: Be prepared for Satan's lies being whispered in your ear today.

Verse of the day: 1 Peter 5:8 {The Message} ~"Keep a cool head. Stay alert. The Devil is poised to pounce, and would like nothing better than to catch you napping. Keep your guard up. You're not the only ones plunged into these hard times. It's the same with Christians all over the world. So keep a firm grip on the faith. The suffering won't last forever. It won't be long before this generous God who has great plans for us in Christ—eternal and glorious plans they are!—will have you put together and on your feet for good. He gets the last word; yes, he does."

Prayer of the day: Dear God, please help me to look out for evil around me. In Jesus's name, I pray. Amen.

THANKSGIVING

Devotion of the day: Take nothing for granted. Sometimes we focus on the things we do not have rather than be happy with the things we have been blessed with. Eve struggled with this as well. Satan tempted Eve in the Garden of Eden by showing her the one thing she was not allowed to have; however, the garden possessed numerous and beautiful kinds of fruits that God had given her. This negative thinking blinded her from the wonderful gifts that were in her reach. Enjoy life and focus on the gifts God has bestowed to you. Look for the countless wonders God has done for you. Walk in the presence of Jesus's light, and this will help you with being grateful.

Challenge of the day: Instead of looking at what is wrong, approach the Lord with thanksgiving for the things that are right.

Verse of the day: 1 John 1:7 (NIV)~" But if we walk in the light, as he is in the light, we have fellowship with one another, and the blood of Jesus, his Son, purifies us from all sins."

Prayer of the day: Dear God, please help me walk in Your light, so I can be more like You everyday. Please put my focus on the amazing sacrifice You did for me instead of the worthless things. In Jesus's name, I pray. Amen.

NOTHING CAN SEPARATE US FROM HIS LOVE

Devotion of the day: You may think nothing is going the way you planned. Maybe you think that your life is unbearable, but if you put God in the situation, everything will fall into place. God is good all the time. You may think He has abandoned you, but He hasn't. He is always with you, no matter what: He loves you no matter what. You are so precious to Him, and He has a plan for your life. Don't give up hope: nothing can separate you from His powerful, unconditional, and everlasting love. I repeat, "nothing".

Challenge of the day: Put God in your situation, and watch how things work out.

Verse of the day: Romans 8:38 (NIV)~"For I am sure that neither death nor life, nor angels nor rulers, nor things present nor things to come, nor powers, nor height nor depth, nor anything else in all creation, will be able to separate us from the love of God in Christ Jesus our Lord."

Prayer of the day: Dear God, thank you for being with me all situations. In Jesus's name, I pray. Amen.

SERVANT'S HEART

Devotion of the day: If you only had one more day to live, what would you do? How would you spend that precious, short time here on earth? That is something we should have in the back of our minds. We don't know how long we will live. All we can do is live and love to the fullest, and do everything for God. Life is so short and should be taken seriously by living like God and not being selfish. Live for God, not yourself: have a servant's heart; serve others and your Lord with a cheerful attitude. The world doesn't revolve around you. The world revolves because of God.

Challenge of the day: Live today like it is your last. Serve others.

Verse of the day: Philippians 2:3-4 {The Message}~"If you've gotten anything at all out of following Christ, if his love has made any difference in your life, if being in a community of the Spirit means anything to you, if you have a heart, if you care— then do me a favor: Agree with each other, love each other, be deep-spirited friends. Don't push your way to the front; don't sweet-talk your way to the top. Put yourself aside, and help others get ahead. Don't be obsessed with getting your own advantage. Forget yourselves long enough to lend a helping hand."

Prayer of the day: Dear God, please help me to be a servant for others in order to show your love. In Jesus's name, I pray. Amen.

GOD MADE EVERYTHING BEAUTIFUL

Devotion of the day: Look how God creates things for the better: caterpillars change into beautiful butterflies; coal into diamonds; sand into pearls. With time you spend with God, you transform into something beautiful. He is working on you and desires for you to live like Him. Trust that God has a perfect plan for your life. He is molding and shaping you into the man and women of God you were designed to be. This transformation may not happen instantly, but this is a beautiful and life-changing process.

Challenge of the day: Have confidence in what God is doing in your life.

Verse of the day: Ecclesiastes 3:11 {The Message}~ "God made everything beautiful in itself and in its time—but he's left us in the dark, so we can never know what God is up to, whether he's coming or going. I've decided that there's nothing better to do than go ahead and have a good time and get the most we can out of life. That's it—eat, drink, and make the most of your job. It's God's gift."

Prayer of the day: Dear God, please help me to have confidence in what you are doing in my life. In Jesus's name, I pray. Amen.

YOU WERE CREATED TO CREATE

Devotion of the day: You were created to create. You were created to do a certain task, maybe even change the world. God placed you on this earth to be put into action, not to just lay back and do nothing. You were created to do something. It doesn't matter how young or how old you are: you are part of God's wonderful plan for the whole world. That's why you are here. He has a dream for you. Your life is in the hands of the maker of Heaven. You are capable of making a difference and to be a light to others. Through you, God can be present, which means love, peace, joy, and victory. Heaven is watching over you and can't wait to see what you will do with your life. Be spontaneous; extraordinary; unique. Lead others to Christ through the talents and abilities God has blessed you with. Change the world while you are still here, because you don't know how much longer you have left here. Make the most of it. You were created to create Jesus's love and light.

Challenge of the day: Today, use your gifts to bring your glory to God and create light to this world.

Verse of the day: Ephesians 2:10 {The Message}~ "Now God has us where he wants us, with all the time in this world and the next to shower grace and kindness upon us in Christ Jesus. Saving is all his idea, and all his work. All we do is trust him enough to let him do it. It's God's gift from start to finish! We don't play the major role. If we did, we'd probably go around bragging that we'd done the whole thing! No, we neither make nor save ourselves. God does both the making and saving. He creates each of us by Christ Jesus to join him in the work he does, the good work he has gotten ready for us to do, work we had better be doing."

Prayer of the day: Dear God, please help me to use my abilities you have blessed me with to lead others to you. Thank you for making me uniquely me. In Jesus's name, I pray. Amen.

TRUE JOY

Devotion of the day: Joy; the kind of happiness of utter bliss: not possessing the newest trend, but knowing that Jesus loves you unconditionally. That's true joy. It's not temporary; it's eternal. In all circumstances, God loves you and fills you with joy to feel His presence. To be joyful, put Jesus in the center of your life and serve others over your own selfish ambitions.

Challenge of the day: Be joyful.

Verse of the day: Psalm 126:3 (NIV)~ "The Lord has done great things for us, and we are filled with joy."

Prayer of the day: Dear God, let me joyful today and reflect your living light. In Jesus's name, I pray. Amen.

CHRIST'S REPRESENTATIVES

Devotion of the day: A Christian who lives like an ambassador is a person who discovers that God has blessed him or her with a gift, and has placed them in this world to represent the kingdom of heaven. Seek to increase the kingdom of God by allowing Christ in your life. Be an example to those around you. Look at life in a different way than the world. You don't represent yourself; you represent Jesus Christ.

Challenge of the day: Be an example of Christ today.

Verse of the day: 2 Corinthians 5:20 {The Message}~ "God has given us the task of telling everyone what he is doing. We're Christ's representatives. God uses us to persuade men and women to drop their differences and enter into God's work of making things right between them. We're speaking for Christ himself now: Become friends with God; he's already a friend with you."

Prayer of the day: Dear God, help me to be an example of Your love each and every day. In Jesus's name, I pray. Amen.

LEAVE A LEGACY

Devotion of the day: Who do you want to be remembered as? That's a question we often have to ask ourselves. Do we want to be remembered as the person who was hateful to others or the person who was joyful and influential? It is ultimately your choice. Ask God to help you be more like Him everyday. If so, you will be the person you desire for people to remember you as. Leave a positive legacy for God's glory.

Challenge of the day: Be the person you would want to be remembered as.

Verse of the day: John 17:1 (NIV)~ "After Jesus said this, he looked toward heaven and prayed: 'Father, the hour has come. Glorify your Son, so that your Son may glorify you.'"

Prayer of the day: Dear God, please help me to leave a legacy not only to others around me, but to the world. In Jesus's name, I pray. Amen.

I WILL FEAR NO EVIL

Devotion of the day: God doesn't want us to worry. Is it even possible to not worry? As God's beloveds, we are called to faith, not fear. Faith says, "God is in charge of my life; I will trust Him, even when circumstances might seem like He's not there. I believe God loves me and knows what is best for me. He has a plan. Even though I don't know exactly what that plan is, I'll have faith."

Challenge of the day: Be fearless.

Verse of the day: Psalm 23:4 (NIV)~ "Even though I walk through the darkest valley, I will fear no evil, for you are with me; your rod and your staff, they comfort me."

Prayer of the day: Dear God, please help me to not worry, but instead give you my worries in exchange for peace and faith. In Jesus's name, I pray. Amen.

ETCHED ON THE CHAMBERS OF YOUR HEART

Devotion of the day: Our goal here is to live like Christ and to draw near to Him. Don't think you have to memorize everything to pass a Bible trivia quiz. You just need to have a relationship with Christ and bury His word deep into your heart. Instead of memorizing, mediate.

Challenge of the day: Mediate on a scripture that speaks to you by repeating it out loud, and have the words and power wash over you.

Verse of the day: Proverbs 7:3 {The Message}~"Dear friend, do what I tell you; treasure my careful instructions. Do what I say and you'll live well. My teaching is as precious as your eyesight—guard it! Write it out on the back of your hands; etch it on the chambers of your heart."

Prayer of the day: Dear God, please help me to read your word and put your word in my heart, so it is always with me. In Jesus's name, I pray. Amen.

RADIANCE

Devotion of the day: When you are with Jesus, you are going to change. People will notice: you will glow, and you will be filled with God's love and truth. For some people, your radiance will be too bright for them. If this happens to you, don't let anyone change your relationship and fire for God. Don't let anyone dim your light.

Challenge of the day: Shine your light today!

Verse of the day: Exodus 34:29 (NIV)~ "He was not aware that his face was radiant because he had spoken with the Lord."

Prayer of the day: Dear God, I want others to notice and recognize that I love you. In Jesus's name, I pray. Amen.

MODESTY

Devotion of the day: Everything you do should be for God's glory; that also includes your clothes. Be aware of what you wear because you are supposed to represent Christ, not the latest trends in this world. Next time you go shopping, look at the clothes for Jesus's standards. Ask yourself, "Would I be comfortable wearing this outfit in front of God?"

Challenge of the day: Analyze your wardrobe, and check if you need to do some cleaning-out.

Verse of the day: 1 Corinthians 10:31 (NIV)~"So whether you eat or drink or whatever you do, do it all for the glory of God."

Prayer of the day: Dear God, let everything I do be for your glory. Let that also include my wardrobe. In Jesus's name, I pray. Amen.

STAND FIRM

Devotion of the day: Negativity is the devil whispering in your ear. When you are negative and complain, that's the devil and not God. When you are insecure and doubt your worth, that's the devil telling you lies. Don't believe them! Ask God to drive the devil out of your path, and God will do it. Stand firm.

Challenge of the day: Recognize when the devil is trying to tell lies and when

God is trying to tell you the truth.

Verse of the day: Ephesians 6:14 (NIV)~ "Stand firm then, with the belt of truth buckled around your waist, with the breastplate of righteousness in place."

Prayer of the day: Dear God, help me to stand firm in my faith in you. In Jesus's name, I pray. Amen.

BITTER DISCONTENT

Devotion of the day: Annoying is a word overused in this culture. Maybe the problem is that not everyone is irritating and bothersome, but maybe it's you. Maybe you are letting the small stuff get to you. Be wise and just blow off comments or actions that bother you: be the bigger person. Don't worry about the person annoying you, but worry about just being you. In doing so, God will look at His son or daughter and say, "I'm so proud of you. Keep on being the light."

Challenge of the day: Be the bigger person today, and don't let the small stuff irritate you.

Verse of the day: Hebrews 12:14 {The Message}~ "Work at getting along with each other and with God. Otherwise you'll never get so much as a glimpse of God. Make sure no one gets left out of God's generosity. Keep a sharp eye out for weeds of bitter discontent. A thistle or two gone to seed can ruin a whole garden in no time. Watch out for the Esau syndrome: trading away God's lifelong gift in order to satisfy a short-term appetite. You well know how Esau later regretted that impulsive act and wanted God's blessing—but by then it was too late, tears or no tears."

Prayer of the day: Dear God, please help me to be the bigger person, and please help me to not focus on

the messes, but remember how I am blessed. In Jesus's
name, I pray. Amen.

GOD WANTS US

Devotion of the day: You are so dearly loved: you are irreplaceable; you are precious. Don't let anyone tell you any different. You were created by the Creator of the entire universe. You are perfect just the way you are. You have a purpose here on this earth. Don't give up, because God loves you. Look at all of creation around you. Beautiful, isn't it? God created all of those beautiful things, but He desires to have a relationship with you.

Challenge of the day: Look at God's beautiful creation today.

Verse of the day: Leviticus 26:12 (NIV)~ "I will walk among you and be your God, and you will be my people."

Prayer of the day: Dear God, Your creation is so beautiful, and I can't believe out of all of that, you desire to have my heart. In Jesus's name, I pray. Amen.

BUCKET-FILLER

Devotion of the day: God fills our buckets, and we overflow with His love. We should share that same love with others, and strive to fill people's buckets with positivity and love instead of emptying their buckets with negativity and hate. Use God's joy to give that same joy to others.

Challenge of the day: Fill someone's bucket today, and have his or her day overflow with happiness from the Lord.

Verse of the day: Proverbs 3:10 {The Message}~ "Trust God from the bottom of your heart; don't try to figure out everything on your own. Listen for God's voice in everything you do, everywhere you go; he's the one who will keep you on track. Don't assume that you know it all. Run to God! Run from evil! Your body will glow with health, your very bones will vibrate with life! Honor God with everything you own; give him the first and the best. Your barns will burst, your wine vats will brim over. But don't, dear friend, resent God's discipline; don't sulk under his loving correction. It's the child he loves that God corrects; a father's delight is behind all this."

Prayer of the day: Dear God, please help me to use Your joy to be a light to others. In Jesus's name, I pray. Amen.

JESUS PAID IT ALL

Devotion of the day: God sent Jesus to pay the price for our sins by sacrificing His life. As a result, those who believe in Christ will have eternal life with Him in heaven. Jesus paid it all, and we received something we didn't deserve: we received God's grace. He washed our crimson stains of sin and purified us white as snow. To receive God in your life, confess that He is God; believe that Jesus died on the cross for your sins, and is God's son, and that He created you and loves you.

Challenge of the day: Read about God's grace in 2 Corinthians 9:8.

Verse of the day: Hebrews 4:16 (NIV)~ "Let us approach the throne of grace with confidence, so that we may receive mercy and find grace to help us in our time of need."

Prayer of the day: Dear God, thank you for sending Your only Son to die on the cross for my sins. I didn't deserve this grace, but this action shows me how much You love me and everyone else You created. Jesus, thank you for paying it all. In Jesus's name, I pray. Amen.

LET YOUR LIGHT SHINE

Devotion of the day: You can impact others. You don't have to go on a mission trip to make a difference in people's lives: you are on a mission trip right now. This is not your permanent home; you belong in heaven. So, you are here. You are right where you are supposed to be, to serve those in your own town. Be a light. Make that your mission in life. The little actions you do here may seem pointless, or not important, but God created you to help those who need some Jesus in their lives. You are exactly where you are supposed to be. Escape the ordinary ways of the world, and be like Jesus, a light.

Challenge of the day: Make your life here on earth a mission trip, in and of itself, by serving those in need.

Verse of the day: Matthew 5:16 (NIV)~"In the same way, let your light shine before others, that they may see your good deeds and glorify your Father in heaven."

Prayer of the day: Dear God, let Your light shine through me, so they can see You. In Jesus's, name, I pray. Amen.

DO LIFE BIG

Devotion of the day: Live to your fullest potential. Let everything you say or do glorify God. Be bold, and do life big! Slow down, and look at all of the beauty around you. Spend every last second of your day loving your Lord and living with a joyful heart. Serve with a heart for the Lord; love others, even when it is difficult; put God and others before yourself; go to God first for everything; pray without ceasing; and, ultimately, have a steadfast desire for God. That's how you do life big.

Challenge of the day: Live life to the fullest.

Verse of the day: Psalm 16:11 (ESV)~"You make known to me the path of life; in your presence there is fullness of joy; at your right hand are pleasures forevermore."

Prayer of the day: Dear God, please help me to do life big and for your glory. In Jesus's name, I pray. Amen.

GREAT WORTH IN GOD'S SIGHT

Devotion of the day: Society says: being beautiful/ handsome is the most important thing you can be; what you look on the outside defines you. God says: your inner disposition is the most beautiful thing in all of creation; I created you to shine a light. Many of us think that our appearances are what makes us who we are, but that's not true. Our culture tells us constantly that we have to look this certain way to be attractive. God created us not for our outer looks, but created us for our character to reflect His light through us. When you feel insecure about your appearance, understand that this feeling comes from the enemy trying to make you feel worthless; but in God's eyes, you are His most prized possession.

Challenge of the day: Don't look in the mirror as often as you normally do. Focus on who you truly are on the inside, not outside.

Verse of the day: 1 Peter 3: 3-4 (NIV)~ "Your beauty should not come from outward adornment, such as elaborate hairstyles and the wearing of gold jewelry or fine clothes. Rather, it should be that of your inner self, the unfading beauty of a gentle and quiet spirit, which is of great worth in God's sight."

Prayer of the day: Dear God, please help me to see myself as You see me. Help me to understand that I am not worthless, and help me to realize that I am a prized possession to You. What matters to You is my inner self that was created for Your glory. In Jesus's name, I pray. Amen.

YOU ARE WORTH DYING FOR

Devotion of the day: You may believe that you are hopeless. You may believe you are not special. You may believe that you are not worth dying for. However, Jesus believes that you are worth being beaten, humiliated, bled, and sacrificed for. Not only did He believe it, but Jesus proved it on the cross. Sometimes you think, "God's grace can't reach someone like me. I'm a mess. Who would love me enough to die for me?" The answer is Christ. He loved you so much that He came to earth for you, paid the price for all your sins, and suffered the most painful death just for you. You are so dearly loved.

Challenge of the day: BELIEVE that you are worth dying for!

Verse of the day: 1 Peter 3:18 (NIV)~ "If with heart and soul you're doing good, do you think you can be stopped? Even if you suffer for it, you're still better off. Don't give the opposition a second thought. Through thick and thin, keep your hearts at attention, in adoration before Christ, your Master. Be ready to speak up and tell anyone who asks why you're living the way you are, and always with the utmost courtesy. Keep a clear conscience before God so that when people throw mud at you, none of it will stick. They'll end up realizing that *they're* the ones who need a bath. It's better to suffer for doing good, if that's what God wants, than to be punished for doing bad. That's what Christ did definitively: suffered because of others' sins, the Righteous One for the unrighteous ones. He went through it all—was put to death and then made alive— to bring us to God."

Prayer of the day: Dear God, please help me to believe that I am set free and am someone worth dying for. Jesus, thank you for dying for all of my sins. In Jesus's name, I pray. Amen.

YOU MAKE ME BRAVE

Devotion of the day: God presents things in our lives that we are uncomfortable with. If this uncomfortable project is to serve others or share the gospel, do it for the love of the Lord. It's not all about you: your focus should be on glorifying God, even if it is out of your comfort zone. Go for it, no matter what the odds, because God makes you brave!

Challenge of the day: Do something extraordinary that is out of your comfort zone {examples: talk to someone about God, serve the needy, etc…}.

Verse of the day: Philippians 2:5 (NIV)~ "In your relationships with one another, have the same mindset as Christ Jesus."

Prayer of the day: Dear God, help me to be brave, and to go out of my comfort zone to spread your good news. In Jesus's name, I pray. Amen.

GOD USES YOU

Devotion of the day: Sometimes we forget that our lives have meaning. We just go through the motions of life and don't really make the most of it: but God has placed you here for a reason, and that purpose is to be a light to others. He uses YOU to spread His love to the world. Take that opportunity, and live as an example of Christ every single day. Your heart beats because you were made to make a difference.

Challenge of the day: Realize that your life has meaning and purpose.

Verse of the day: Psalm 57:2 (NIV)~ "I cry out to God Most High, to God who fulfills his purpose for me."

Prayer of the day: Dear God, please help me to find the purpose You have for my life, and use me to spread Your love. In Jesus's name, I pray. Amen.

UNIQUE WILDFLOWERS

Devotion of the day: Wishing for an attribute or ability we do not possess occurs many times in our hearts: but those thoughts are not what God desires. He created us with a definite and planned purpose. The Creator did not make us without reason or meaning. As God's beloved children, we are very similar to flowers. We are all different from each other: we are different colors, smells, and purposes. If every single flower was the same in this world, the world would not be nearly as beautiful. Likewise, if every single person was the same in this world, what would be the point of us being here? So, remember, the next time you wish for hair like someone else, personality, talents, or anything else that you do not have, thank God for what He did bless you with. Without you in this world, it would not be nearly as beautiful or unique.

Challenge of the day: Today, don't wish for an attribute or talent you do not have. Instead, thank God for the talents and attributes you do have.

Verse of the day: Psalm 30:11 {The Message}~ "You did it: you changed wild lament into whirling dance; you ripped off my black mourning band and decked me with wildflowers. I'm about to burst with song; I can't keep quiet about you. God, my God, I can't thank you enough."

Prayer of the day: Dear God, thank you for creating me as unique and beautiful as the wildflowers in this world. In Jesus's name, I pray. Amen.

GREATEST IS LOVE

Devotion of the day: Love is the most important action in the world. Jesus proved His love for us on the cross. To show others how great God is, we need to spread the love of Christ everywhere we go. Loving others is sometimes a difficult task, but if you use your burning desire for God through your action and words, His love will just pour out of you and impact everyone in your path. They will see how joyful and loving you are, and they will desire to be just like that. Now that's how you show the love of Jesus Christ; by just letting Him do all the life-changing while you are a bulb, and Jesus's love is the actual light reflecting through you.

Challenge of the day: Let Jesus have control of the life-changing through you.

Verse of the day: 1 Corinthians 13:3 (NIV)~ "And now these three remain: faith, hope and love. But the greatest of these is love."

Prayer of the day: Dear God, please bring Your love to life inside of me. In Jesus's name, I pray. Amen.

ESCAPE THE ORDINARY

Devotion of the day: Being different from this world can sometimes be a challenge, but you are strong enough to be an example of Christ. In the little actions you do, you have the ability to change a life forever. You may not even realize the impact you are influencing in others around you. Jesus changed numerous lives, and that same power is within you. God uses YOU to spread His love to the whole world. You may think you are too small, too young, too weak, or not good enough, but there is nothing you can't do. God loves you so very much and has created you to be different from this world, so you can reach those who may not know or believe in Him. You can change that. Set the world on fire for God, and escape the ordinary!

Challenge of the day: Escape the ordinary, and be an example of Christ.

Verse of the day: Romans 12:2 (NIV)~ "Don't become so well-adjusted to your culture that you fit into it without even thinking. Instead, fix your attention on God. You'll be changed from the inside out. Readily recognize what he wants from you, and quickly respond to it. Unlike the culture around you, always dragging you down to its level of immaturity, God brings the best out of you, develops well-formed maturity in you."

Prayer of the day: Dear God, thank you for everything you have done for me. Let me be Your messenger to the world and spread Your love. Help me to escape the culture I live in. I love you. In Jesus's name, I pray. Amen.

ABOUT THE AUTHOR

*M*y name is Cameron Grace Mitchell, and I
live in Tulsa, Oklahoma. I accepted Jesus
into my heart when I was just six years old, but that
decision was just the beginning of what God had in
store for me. On January 17, 2014, the Lord put something on my heart. He desired for me to write devotions for my freshmen classmates to encourage and
brighten their day. I would write these devotions in
my notes on my iPhone and text them to everyone I
knew. Interestingly enough, I did not write the devotions. God used His words though me. Before I wrote
a single letter, I prayed to God to give me the words
He wanted me to share. Little did I know that this
small action could do some big things. Many people
responded and said, "I really needed this today" or
"This made my day". My classmates' reactions to my
devotions were God's way of telling me that I was,
and I am still, making an impact on the lives around
me for God's glory. I realized that I am not too young
to do life big. Just sending a positive text message can
influence how someone's day goes. I challenge you to

show God's love in everything you do. Let God get the glory through the actions you do for others. You CAN make a difference. Just let God do all the work through you. You are God's vessel to touch people, and you have the power to change and transform hearts, no matter what age you are. Live for Christ and escape the ordinary ways of this world. Just because you live in the world does not mean you have to be of it. Let your little light shine.

Matthew 5:14~ "You are the light of the world. A city on a hill can not be hidden."

Follow my blog for even more devotions and positive messages! escapetheordinaryblog.wordpress.com

BIBLE COPYRIGHT

New International Version – Matthew 5:14, Psalm 119:37, Song of Solomon 2:16, Song of Solomon 8:67, 1 Peter 5:7, Jeremiah 29:11, 1 Peter 2:16, Luke 10:27, James 4:8, Ephesians 4:29, Proverbs 4:23, Psalm 91:4, Proverbs 14:30, Romans 5:8, Romans 8:28, John 13:34-35, Ephesians 3:18, Isaiah 40:31, 2 Corinthians 5:7, 1 John 4:19, 1 Thessalonians 5;16-18. 2 Corinthians 5:17, Matthew 6:6, Psalm 46:5, Proverbs 16:9, 1 Timothy 4:12, Philippians 3:13-14, Psalm 138:8, Isaiah 41:10, Exodus 14:14, 1 Thessalonians 5:17, Psalm 107:1, Psalm 37:4-5, Colossians 3:23, Romans 12:21, John 3:30, John 8:7, Matthew 5:11, Matthew 11:28-30, 1 John 1:7, Romans 8:38, John 17:1, Psalm 23:4, Exodus 34:29, 1 Corinthians 10:31, Ephesians 6:14, Hebrews 4:16, Matthew 5:16, 1 Peter 3:3-4, 1 Peter 3;18, Philippians 2:5, Psalm 57:2, 1 Corinthians 13:3, Psalm 118:24, Romans 12:2

The Message – Mark 4:38-39, Song of Solomon 6:10, Philippians 3:14, 1 Peter 5:8, Philippians 2:3-4, Ecclesiastes 3:11, Ephesians 2:10, 2 Corinthians

5:20, Proverbs 7:3, Hebrews 12:14, Leviticus 26:12, Proverbs 3:10, Psalm 30:11

English Standard Version– Psalm 16:11

New Living Version– Deuteronomy 31:6